Mark Twain

The Adventures of Tom Sawyer

Illustrated by **Fabio Delvò**
Text adaptation and activities by
Gina D. B. Clemen

Member of CISQ Federation

CERTIFIED MANAGEMENT SYSTEM
ISO 9001

The design, production and distribution of educational materials for the CIDEB (Black Cat) brand are managed in compliance with the rules of Quality Management System which fulfils the requirements of the standard ISO 9001

Content editor: Maria Grazia Donati
Editor: Chiara Versino
Design: Sara Fabbri, Silvia Bassi
Page Layout: Annalisa Possenti
Picture research: Alice Graziotin

Art Director: Nadia Maestri

© 2017 Black Cat
First edition: February 2017

DEALINK, DEAFLIX are trademarks licensed by De Agostini SpA

Picture credits:
Shutterstock; iStockphoto; Dreamstime; Michael DeFreitas North America / Alamy Stock Photo: 5; Bettmann / Getty Images: 50; Bridgeman Images: 53; DeAgostini Picture Library: 70 (5a, 5c); World History Archive / AGF: (5b).

All rights reserved. No part of this book may be reproduced, stored in a retrieval system or transmitted, in any form or by any means, electronic, mechanical, photocopying, recording or otherwise, without the written permission of the publisher.

We would be happy to give you further information concerning our material and receive your comments.

info@blackcat-cideb.com
blackcat-cideb.com

Printed in Italy by Italgrafica, Novara

Contents

Mark Twain   4

Before you read   6

The story
Chapter 1	Tom and the fence	9
Chapter 2	Huck Finn	15
Chapter 3	At the graveyard	20
Chapter 4	The adventure on Jackson's Island	25
Chapter 5	The trial	31
Chapter 6	Inside McDougal's Cave	38
Chapter 7	The treasure box	43

Dossiers
Missouri: the door to the West	49
Native American Indians	52

Activities   55

n. track 🔊 THE STORY IS FULLY RECORDED.

Mark Twain

Mark Twain is often called the father of American literature. He changed the American way of writing with his simple, funny language. Everyone could understand and enjoy his stories, and his books became popular everywhere.

Mark Twain's real name was Samuel Langhorne Clemens. He was born in Florida, Missouri, on November 30, 1835. In 1839 he and his family went to live in Hannibal, Missouri, a small town on the Mississippi River. Young Samuel grew up there, and as a boy he had many adventures on the river with his friends.

He began working as a steamboat [1] pilot on the Mississippi River in 1857, and he liked his job. In 1861 he went to the West and he traveled to Nevada and then to California. He went to Virginia City, Nevada, to look for gold and silver, but he didn't find much. So he decided to work as a journalist for the *Territorial Enterprise*. Today you can visit the Mark Twain Museum in Virginia City and see his old desk and other interesting things.

1. steamboat :

In San Francisco, California, he began working as a journalist for *The Morning Call*. Here he changed his name to Mark Twain. When he worked as a steamboat pilot the term "Mark Twain" meant "safe water ahead". In 1865 he wrote the short story "The Celebrated Jumping Frog of Calaveras County", and it was a great success. He became a famous writer and he traveled to different places in the world.

Desk and painting at the Mark Twain Museum, Virginia City, Nevada.

In 1870 he married Olivia "Livy" Langdon and they had three daughters and a son. The family lived in Hartford, Connecticut. Here Mark Twain wrote his three famous books: *The Adventures of Tom Sawyer* (1876), *Life on the Mississippi* (1883) and *Adventures of Huckleberry Finn* (1884).

His other great books are *The Prince and the Pauper* (1881), *The Innocents Abroad* (1869), *A Connecticut Yankee in King Arthur's Court* (1889), and many short stories. His wonderful books are translated into more than 70 languages!

Mark Twain died on April 21, 1910 at the age of seventy-four.

COMPREHENSION CHECK

1. Are the following sentences true (T) or false (F)? Correct the false ones.

	T	F
1. People everywhere liked his simple, funny language.	☐	☐
2. Mark Twain's real name was Samuel Langhorne Clemens.	☐	☐
3. He was born in Hannibal, Missouri.	☐	☐
4. He worked on a farm near the Mississippi River.	☐	☐
5. In San Francisco he worked as a journalist.	☐	☐
6. His first short story was published in 1865.	☐	☐
7. Mark Twain and his family lived in Nevada.	☐	☐

BEFORE YOU READ

1. Match the words with the correct picture.

cross • frying pan • cave • brush • bark • jail • fence • kite • rifle • graveyard • ghost • rat • beetle • treasure • haunted house • pirate • coins • hang • candle • bat • witch

1 ....
2 ....
3 ....
4 ....
5 ....
6 ....
7 ....
8 ....
9 ....
10 ....
11 ....
12 ....

BEFORE YOU READ

13 .... 14 .... 15 ....

16 .... 17 .... 18 ....

19 .... 20 .... 21 ....

2. Match the words with the correct meaning. Use a dictionary if necessary.

1. ☐ tricks   a to make a hole in the ground
2. ☐ meow   b a long passage under the ground
3. ☐ robber   c a person who advises people on legal problems
4. ☐ to dig   d the sound a cat makes
5. ☐ proud   e you know who the person is when you see him/her
6. ☐ to drown   f to speak very softly
7. ☐ lawyer   g to die in the water
8. ☐ tunnel   h little games, jokes
9. ☐ to recognize   i a person who steals things from other people
10. ☐ to whisper   j satisfied and happy

THE CHARACTERS

From left to right, first row: **Becky Thatcher**, **Tom Sawyer**, **Huck Finn**.
Second row: **Aunt Polly**, **Muff Potter**, **Injun Joe**.

CHAPTER 1

Tom and the fence

"Tom! Tom!"

There was no answer.

"Where is that boy? Tom!" cried Aunt Polly, who was a kind woman with white hair and glasses. She was tall and thin, but she had big hands. She looked under the bed but she only found the old cat.

"Tom!" she cried again. She went to the kitchen and opened the door to the garden and looked around.

Suddenly she heard a noise behind her. A small boy ran past her and she stopped him with her big hand.

"Tom! What are you doing?" she asked.

"Nothing, Aunt Polly," said Tom.

"Nothing?" said Aunt Polly. "Look at your hands and your mouth. You were eating jam! How many times did I tell you: *don't eat the jam!*"

"Oh, Aunt Polly... look behind you!" said Tom excitedly.

CHAPTER 1

Aunt Polly turned around and Tom quickly ran away. She was surprised and then she laughed softly.

"Tom always plays tricks on me and I never learn," said Aunt Polly to herself. "I love him, but it's not easy to look after him. He's my sister's child – she's dead. Now I have to teach him to be a good boy." She went back to the kitchen and thought about Tom.

"Tomorrow's Saturday and there's no school," she thought. "Tom must work tomorrow. He hates work and loves to play. But he must learn to work, and I have the right thing for him to do. He can paint the fence!"

Tom lived in the town of St Petersburg with his Aunt Polly and his brother Sid. During the long summer evenings there weren't a lot of fun things to do. Tom liked walking around town. One evening he met a big boy who was a stranger. Tom looked at him because he didn't see new people often. The boy had new, expensive clothes.

"Who is this boy?" Tom thought. "He's got new shoes, a blue jacket, a white shirt, a brown hat and a blue tie, … but it's not Sunday. He probably comes from a big city. My clothes are really old and ugly, and I don't have any shoes."

They looked at each other – Tom didn't like him.

Tom finally said, "I can beat you!" [1]

The big boy laughed and said, "Why don't you try?"

There was a moment of silence.

"What's your name?" asked Tom.

"I'm not going to tell you," answered the big boy.

"Oh, really," said Tom nervously.

"I think you're afraid of me," said the big boy. "I'm bigger and stronger than you."

"I'm not afraid of you," said Tom. "I'm not afraid of anyone!"

There was another moment of silence. The two boys looked at each other angrily.

Suddenly Tom pushed the boy and the boy pushed Tom. Soon they were fighting on the ground. Tom hit him and pulled his hair. Then the

---

1. beat you : win in a fight.

big boy hit Tom on the nose but this didn't stop him. Soon the big boy started crying and said, "Stop! Stop!"

Tom got up from the ground and said, "Well, I said I could beat you, didn't I?" The big boy's nice clothes were dirty and he got up slowly and walked away.

When Tom got home Aunt Polly said, "Tom, you're late! And look at your clothes – they're terribly dirty! You'll never learn. Now go to bed! Tomorrow's Saturday…"

Everyone was happy on Saturday morning, but not Tom. He sat in front of a high fence and looked at it sadly. It was nine feet [2] high and ninety feet [3] long.

"This is terrible," thought Tom, sitting under a big tree. "It's a beautiful Saturday morning and I must paint the fence. My friends are going swimming and fishing, and I'm sitting here in front of this fence. They're all going to laugh at me."

He got up slowly and went to get the brush and the paint. He put the long brush in the white paint and started painting. After a few minutes he stopped and looked at his work. Then he continued painting and he was very unhappy.

Suddenly he had a great idea. His friend Ben Rogers was walking down the street and he was eating a big red apple. He saw Tom and said, "It's Saturday and you're working for your Aunt Polly."

2. **nine feet :** about 3 meters.
3. **ninety feet :** about 28 meters.

Tom continued to paint and didn't say a word.

"Tom, I'm going swimming in the river, but you can't come with me," said Ben Rogers. "You're working."

"Do you call this *work*?" said Tom, who continued to paint.

"You're painting your aunt's fence," said Ben, "of course it's work."

"Well, maybe it's work but maybe it isn't," said Tom. "I like it! I can go swimming every day, but I can't paint a fence every day."

Ben was surprised and he watched Tom. He painted slowly and carefully, and he often smiled. He stopped and moved back from the fence. He looked at his work and was happy. Ben wanted to paint, too.

"Listen Tom, let me paint a little," said Ben. "I want to try."

Tom looked at Ben and said, "I'm really sorry, Ben, but Aunt Polly wants me to do it. You know, I'm very good at painting. My brother Sid wanted to do it, but he's not good at painting."

"Oh, Tom, let me try, please!" said Ben. "I'll be careful."

"No, Ben, this is an important job," said Tom. "Only I can do it".

"Here, you can have some of my apple…" said Ben.

"No, no!" said Tom, who continued to paint slowly and carefully.

"Well, then take *all* of my apple!" said Ben excitedly.

Tom was happy but he didn't smile. "Alright, Ben, you can paint for a short time."

Tom gave Ben the long brush and he sat down under the big tree and ate the apple.

That morning Tom's other friends came by.

Billy Fisher saw him painting and laughed at him.

CHAPTER 1

"I'm going fishing, but you can't come with me because you're working." Then Billy Fisher watched Tom paint and suddenly he wanted to try, too.

"Tom, let me paint the fence," said Billy Fisher. "I'll give you my new kite!"

So Billy Fisher started to paint the fence and Tom sat down and looked at his new kite. Then Johnny Miller came along and wanted to paint the fence, too. He gave Tom a big dead rat. His other friends came by and wanted to paint the fence. They gave him a cat with one eye, an old knife, an old blue bottle, a key and some other things. Tom's friends painted the big fence while Tom sat under the big tree. He looked at all the interesting things his friends gave him and thought, "When something is difficult to get, everyone wants it."

When the fence was painted he went back home and said, "The work's done, Aunt Polly. Can I go out and play with my friends?"

"I want to see the fence first," said Aunt Polly. She went out and looked at the beautiful white fence and smiled at Tom, "You did a very good job. Here, take this big red apple and go and play!"

Read the sentence below taken from this chapter.

"It's a beautiful Saturday morning and I must paint the fence. My friends are going swimming and fishing, and I'm sitting in front of this fence."

Tom doesn't want to paint the fence and he makes his friends believe that painting the fence is fun.
Circle the words below that describe Tom.

lazy • honest • clever • kind • smart • funny • friendly • stupid • intelligent

UNDERSTANDING THE TEXT • page 56
MAPPING VALUES AND FEELINGS • page 78

CHAPTER 2

Huck Finn

Sunday was the next day. Tom didn't like Sunday because he and Sid had to go to Sunday school. He had to wear his Sunday clothes and he hated them because they were uncomfortable. On Sundays he had to comb his hair and wear shoes, too. Sid liked going to Sunday school, but Tom didn't. Sunday school started at nine o'clock and ended at half past ten. He never listened to the teacher and he made noises.

After Sunday school Tom and Sid went to church with Aunt Polly. There were usually more than one hundred people in church on Sunday. Tom was always bored and wanted to have some fun. He brought a big black beetle in his pocket and took it out when the reverend started speaking. He put the black beetle on the floor of the church and it started walking around.

When a little dog in the church saw the beetle it ran after it. Suddenly the beetle bit the dog's nose and the dog started to bark loudly.

CHAPTER 2

It ran around the church and made a lot of noise. Everyone was very surprised. The reverend continued speaking but no one listened to him. The people in the church looked at the dog and the beetle and laughed silently. Tom was happy because he had an interesting morning in the church!

"It's Monday morning and time for school!" cried Aunt Polly. "Get up immediately, Tom!" The next day was Monday and Tom didn't want to go to school. Tom went to a one-room school, where there were children of different ages.

On his way to school Tom met his good friend Huckleberry Finn. Everyone called him Huck. Huck's father never worked and his mother was dead. He didn't have a home and lived in the streets. He never went to school and his clothes were old and dirty. He went swimming and fishing and was always happy.

The mothers in the town didn't like Huck because he said bad words. All the children of the village liked him very much because he did everything he wanted to do.

"Hello Huck!" said Tom. He was always happy to see Huck.

"Hello Tom!" said Huck. "Are you going to school?"

"Yeah," said Tom sadly, "it's Monday morning. What else can I do? What do you have in that bag?"

"It's a dead cat," said Huck.

"A dead cat!" exclaimed Tom. "What are you going to do with it?"

"Can you keep a secret?" asked Huck.

"Of course I can!" said Tom, looking at the bag.

"Well, I want to take it to the graveyard after midnight," said Huck. "A dead cat can call ghosts out of their graves. It's easier than you think."

"Are you sure?" asked Tom, who was very surprised. "Who told you?"

"Old Mrs Hopkins told me," said Huck. "She's a witch and she knows all about these things."

"This sounds exciting," said Tom. "Can I come with you, Huck?"

"Of course!" said Huck. "Or are you afraid of ghosts?"

"Afraid of ghosts?" said Tom, looking at Huck. "Of course not! Come and call me at my window at eleven o'clock tonight."

Tom was late for school that morning and the teacher was very angry. "Thomas Sawyer! You're late *again*!"

Suddenly Tom saw a new girl in the classroom. She had lovely blue eyes and long blonde hair. She was a pretty girl and Tom liked her a lot. There was a free chair next to her and Tom wanted to sit there. But how could he?

Tom was clever and he thought quickly. "I'm late because I talked to Huckleberry Finn," he said.

"What! You must never talk to that bad boy!" cried the teacher angrily. "Now go and sit with the girls!"

The children in the classroom laughed at Tom. He sat down next to the lovely new girl and he was happy. He drew a picture of a house.

The girl said, "Let me see it."

Tom put the picture in front of her.

"It's a good picture," she said. "Now draw a man."

Tom drew a man near the house. It was a terrible picture but the girl liked it.

"Oh, you know how to draw," she said. "I can't draw."

"I can teach you after school," said Tom.

"That's very nice of you," said the girl, smiling at him. She was friendly.

"What's your name?" Tom asked.

"Becky Thatcher," she said. "I already know your name – it's Tom Sawyer." Tom looked at Becky and smiled.

Tom and Sid went to bed at half past nine that night. Sid fell asleep immediately but Tom didn't. He was waiting for Huck.

At eleven o'clock Huck made a strange noise – the meow of a cat. Tom got dressed and went out of the bedroom window.

"Are you ready, Tom?" asked Huck, who was holding the dead cat.

"Yeah, let's go!" answered Tom.

They walked down a dark road for about thirty minutes. It was a warm night and there was a big moon in the night sky. The graveyard was on a hill and there were a lot of trees and graves. The wind made scary noises.

Huck Finn

Tom was afraid but he didn't say anything to Huck. "This place is probably full of ghosts," he thought.

"Let's look for the grave of Hoss Williams," said Huck, as they walked through the graveyard. "Look, here it is! He died last week."

"Do… do you think Hoss Williams can hear us?" asked Tom.

"I think his ghost can hear us," said Huck.

"Let's call him *Mr.* Williams, then," said Tom.

"But everyone in St Petersburg called him Hoss," said Huck.

"Quiet!" said Tom.

"What's the matter?" asked Huck.

"Do you hear that noise? Look over there… oh, no!" said Tom. His heart was beating fast and his face was hot.

 THINK!

The mothers in St Petersburg don't like Huck. He's *different* from all the other children in town.
What can you do when you meet someone who is *different* from you and others? Choose one answer.

- a ☐ Laugh at him/her
- b ☐ Make friends and be kind to him/her
- c ☐ Don't talk to him/her

UNDERSTANDING THE TEXT • page 58
MAPPING VALUES AND FEELINGS • page 78

CHAPTER 3

At the graveyard

"I can see ghosts, real ghosts!" said Huck. "They're coming here! I'm really scared, Tom."

"Oh, no!" said Tom. "Can they see us?"

"Ghosts can see everything and everyone," said Huck. "Why did I come here?"

"Let's be very quiet," said Tom. "Don't be scared, Huck. We're here together."

The two boys quickly hid behind a big tree. The three ghosts moved around the graveyard and didn't make any noise. They came close to Tom and Huck.

Suddenly Huck exclaimed, "They're not ghosts – they're people! One of them is Muff Potter."

"You're right," said Tom, looking at the three men. "I can see Doctor Robinson and Injun [1] Joe. But what are they doing here at night?"

"Those men are grave robbers," said Huck. "They want to steal a dead body from a grave."

"But why?" asked Tom, who didn't understand.

"The doctor wants a dead body," said Huck. "He cuts the bodies and studies them. My father told me about Doctor Robinson."

The three men were standing by Hoss Williams's grave. Muff Potter and Injun Joe started to dig and soon the grave was open. They found the dead body and pulled it out of the ground. Tom and Huck watched them from behind the big tree.

"Well, Dr Robinson, do you want us to take the body to your house?" asked Muff.

"Yes, of course," said Doctor Robinson.

---

1. **Injun :** a Native American Indian. Injun was the local pronunciation of Indian.

CHAPTER 3

"Then you must give us five dollars," said Muff.

"But I paid you early this morning," said Doctor Robinson. "Don't you remember? I'm not giving you any more money!"

Injun Joe looked at Doctor Robinson angrily and said, "I want more money, doctor. Five years ago I came to your father's house. I asked you for something to eat but you gave me nothing. I still remember that. Now give me more money!"

Injun Joe was a big, strong American Indian. He took the doctor's arm and the doctor hit him. Injun Joe fell to the ground.

"Don't hit my friend!" cried Muff Potter, who hit Doctor Robinson. Soon Muff and the doctor were fighting on the ground.

Dr Robinson was angry and hit Muff Potter on the head. Muff fell to the ground and didn't move. Then Injun Joe took Muff's knife. He turned around and looked angrily at Dr Robinson, lifted Muff's knife and killed the doctor! Tom and Huck watched the horrible scene and were very scared.

Injun Joe looked at the two men on the ground near Hoss Williams's grave. He took all the money out of the doctor's pockets and then put the bloody knife into Muff's right hand.

After a few minutes Muff opened his eyes and pushed the doctor's body away. He looked at the knife in his right hand and didn't know what happened.

"Joe, what... what happened?" asked Muff slowly. "Why is this bloody knife in my hand?"

"Muff, you... you killed the doctor!" said Injun Joe.

"What!" exclaimed Muff, dropping the knife. "I didn't kill him, Joe. I... I can't remember anything... my head hurts. Joe, tell me what happened."

"You fought with the doctor," said Injun Joe. "Do you remember that?"

"Yeah, I remember that," said Muff, looking at his friend. "I wanted more money and the doctor got angry."

"The doctor hit you on the head and you fell to the ground," explained Injun Joe. "Then you got up, took your knife and killed him. That's what happened."

"I don't understand," said Muff. "I never fight with a knife – never. I didn't want to kill the doctor. This is terrible! Joe, please don't tell anyone."

CHAPTER 3

"I'm your friend, Muff," said Injun Joe. "I won't tell anyone. But now you must leave the graveyard. Go back home, quickly. It's dark and nobody will see you."

"Thank you, Joe," said Muff, leaving. "You're a real friend."

When Muff left the graveyard, Injun Joe put Muff's knife near the doctor's body and ran away down the hill.

Tom and Huck were very frightened. They saw all the terrible things that happened. They moved away from behind the big tree, where they were hiding. They ran out of the graveyard and back to the town. They saw an old house near the river and decided to hide there.

"Now what are we going to do, Huck?" asked Tom. "Injun Joe killed Doctor Robinson."

"Well, we can't tell anyone," said Huck.

"But we saw everything," said Tom.

"Injun Joe's a dangerous man," said Huck. "Everyone's afraid of him, you know that. Do you want a knife in your heart?"

"No!" cried Tom, who was scared.

"Promise not to tell anyone!" said Huck.

"I promise, Huck," said Tom. "I promise."

THINK!

Muff thinks Injun Joe is a true friend, but he's not!
Read these definitions of *friendship*. Which one do you prefer?

a ☐ A friend is someone who is kind to you.
b ☐ Friends are people who like each other.
c ☐ Two friends are people who enjoy each other's company.
d ☐ A friend is the first person you want to call when you hear good news.

Now write your definition of friendship.

UNDERSTANDING THE TEXT • page 60
MAPPING VALUES AND FEELINGS • page 78

CHAPTER 4

The adventure on Jackson's Island

Everyone in St Petersburg found out about poor Doctor Robinson the next day. The sheriff found Muff Potter's knife near the doctor's body and he put Muff in the town jail.

Tom and Huck were worried. "We saw Injun Joe kill the doctor," said Tom. "Muff didn't kill him and now he's in jail. Poor Muff!"

"I know, Tom," said Huck. "We can't say anything because Injun Joe's a very dangerous man. He could kill us! But I'm really sorry for Muff."

"You're right Huck," said Tom sadly. "We must keep this a secret." The two boys were really afraid of Injun Joe.

Tom couldn't forget the terrible night at the graveyard. He had bad dreams about Injun Joe and Muff Potter. He kept the secret but he was very unhappy.

Aunt Polly was worried about him because he didn't eat much. She gave him a lot of different medicines but Tom didn't feel better. He was

CHAPTER 4

unhappy at school, too. Becky Thatcher didn't talk to him anymore, and he didn't know why.

"My life's terrible," thought Tom. "I have too many problems and no one loves me."

It was now summer and school was over. Tom and Huck were happy and they didn't think about Injun Joe and the terrible night at the graveyard. Every day was hot and sunny, and Tom and his friend Joe Harper went swimming and fishing in the Mississippi River. One day Tom said, "Let's go and do something exciting!"

"Alright," said Joe, who was always interested in Tom's ideas, "but what can we do?"

"Let's run away!" said Tom excitedly. "Let's go and live on Jackson's Island. We can be pirates and have great fun."

Jackson's Island was a small island in the Mississippi River. It was near St Petersburg and no one lived there.

"I'm going to tell Huck, too," said Tom. "He likes exciting adventures."

"Good idea, Tom," said Joe Harper. "Huck is lots of fun."

"Remember, Joe, don't tell your mother, father or anyone about our plan," said Tom. "Go home and bring some food. We can meet here at midnight."

The three boys met on the river at midnight. Tom brought some meat and Joe brought some bread. Huck brought an old frying pan and a knife.

"Do we need anything else?" asked Joe, who was excited about this new adventure.

"No… I don't think so," said Tom, thinking.

They found a small boat and they went down the river to Jackson's Island.

When they got there they made a fire and cooked some meat. They watched the big white steamboats travel on the Mississippi River.

"What great fun!" exclaimed Joe.

"We're free and we can do anything we want," said Tom happily.

"What do pirates do?" asked Huck.

"Pirates go on ships and steal treasure," said Tom. "Then they go to their island and hide it in a secret place."

CHAPTER 4

Jackson's Island was a wonderful place. The three boys were happy there and they slept under the stars.

Tom, Huck and Joe woke up early the next morning. It was a hot day and they went swimming in the river. Then they went fishing and cooked a big fish for breakfast.

"This is the best breakfast in the world!" exclaimed Huck, who was always hungry. The three boys laughed.

They spent the day exploring the island. In the afternoon they sat around the fire and ate some meat and bread. Suddenly Tom said, "Listen! Can you hear that strange noise?"

"What is it?" asked Joe.

"Let's go and see," said Huck.

They ran to the river and saw a big steamboat with a lot of small boats near it.

"Every boat from St Petersburg is out on the river," said Joe. "What's happening?"

"I know!" said Huck. "They're looking for a dead body in the river. The same thing happened last summer when Bill Turner fell into the river and drowned."

Joe was worried and asked, "Who are they looking for this time?"

Tom thought for a moment and said, "They're looking for us! No one knows where we are and everyone thinks we drowned. Remember, we didn't sleep at home last night and we spent the whole day here on Jackson's Island. Everyone's worried."

Tom, Huck and Joe looked at each other and laughed loudly. They felt like heroes.

"Everyone in St Petersburg is talking about us," said Tom happily.

"Hurrah!" cried Huck. "Now we're famous!"

The steamboat and the other boats went away in the evening. Tom, Huck and Joe had a lot of fun on Jackson's Island. They felt like real pirates. That evening they sat around the fire and talked about their adventures. Then they went to sleep, but Tom couldn't sleep.

When Huck and Joe woke up the next morning, Tom wasn't there.

"Where's Tom?" asked Joe. "He's not here."

"I don't know, Joe," said Huck looking around. Suddenly he cried, "Joe, look! Tom's swimming in the river and he's coming here."

Tom came back to Jackson's Island and told them his story.

"Last night I couldn't sleep because I thought about Aunt Polly. So I went home and no one saw me. I saw Aunt Polly and your mother, Joe. They were both crying because they think we're dead. Everyone thinks we're dead. And I heard some interesting things."

"What did you hear?" asked Huck.

Tom looked at his friends and smiled. "There will be a funeral [1] for us on Sunday at the church."

"A funeral for us!" exclaimed Huck and Joe, who started laughing.

"Yeah, a funeral," said Tom. "And now I'll tell you my great idea. Listen!"

Huck and Joe listened to Tom's great idea and liked it.

On Sunday there were no happy faces in St Petersburg. Everyone in town was in the small church for the funeral. Aunt Polly, Sid and Joe Harper's family were all dressed in black. The reverend said many kind words about Tom, Joe and Huck. The boys' families cried and cried. Everyone in the church cried.

Suddenly there was a noise at the church door. The reverend stopped speaking and looked up. Everyone turned around and looked in amazement. The three boys slowly walked into the church. Tom was first, then Joe and then Huck.

---

1. funeral : a ceremony when a person dies.

CHAPTER 4

No one could believe what was happening. The three boys weren't dead – they were alive and well! Aunt Polly and Joe's mother ran to the boys and kissed Tom and Joe. Aunt Polly cried and then she laughed. Poor Huck didn't know what to do. No one kissed him and he started moving away. Tom stopped him.

Tom looked at Aunt Polly and said, "It's not right! Someone must be happy to see Huck."

"You're right, Tom," said Aunt Polly and she kissed Huck, who was very happy.

Tom was proud of his great idea.

The reverend looked at the three boys and smiled. "Tom, Joe and Huck are back with us. Let's sing and be happy!" Everyone sang and it was a very happy Sunday.

THINK!

Read the sentence below taken from this chapter.

Tom said, *"Last night I couldn't sleep because I thought about Aunt Polly."*

Tom knows he didn't do the right thing: he didn't tell Aunt Polly that he was going to Jackson's Island. He was not *considerate*. **A considerate person thinks about the feelings of other people. Aunt Polly is like a mother and she cares about Tom. She loves him and worries about him. Are you** *considerate*? **If you go out with your friends and your parents don't know, what do you do? Choose one answer.**

- a ☐ You write a note and leave it on the kitchen table.
- b ☐ You text one of your parents.
- c ☐ You phone one of your parents.
- d ☐ You do nothing.

UNDERSTANDING THE TEXT • page 62
MAPPING VALUES AND FEELINGS • page 78

CHAPTER 5

The trial[1]

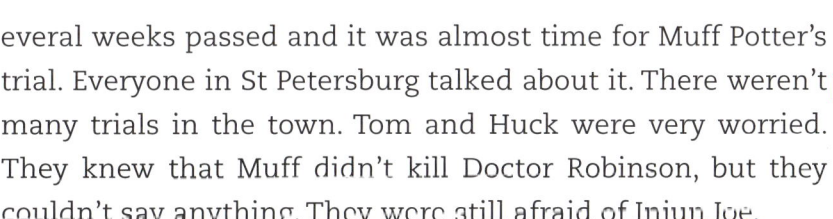

Several weeks passed and it was almost time for Muff Potter's trial. Everyone in St Petersburg talked about it. There weren't many trials in the town. Tom and Huck were very worried. They knew that Muff didn't kill Doctor Robinson, but they couldn't say anything. They were still afraid of Injun Joe.

One morning Tom told Huck, "Meet me on Cardiff Hill at noon. I want to talk to you."

"About what?" asked Huck.

"About – *that*," said Tom.

At noon the two boys met on Cardiff Hill, far away from the town.

"Huck, did you tell anyone about – *that*?" asked Tom, who was worried.

"No, of course not!" said Huck.

"You never said a word to anyone?" asked Tom.

---

1. **trial**: a formal meeting in a law court when people decide if a person is guilty or innocent.

CHAPTER 5

"Never a word!" said Huck. "But why are you asking me?"

"Well, I'm afraid – really afraid of Injun Joe," said Tom.

"I'm afraid of him, too," said Huck. "That's why we have this secret."

"You know, I'm very sorry for old Muff," said Tom. "Everyone in St Petersburg says he's a killer, but it's not true."

"Muff's a kind man," said Huck. "Once he gave me half a fish. Sometimes he sat with me near the river and we talked about fishing."

"And once he helped me with my kite," said Tom. "They're going to hang poor Muff, and we know that he didn't kill Doctor Robinson. Injun Joe killed the doctor!"

"But we can't tell anyone about Injun Joe," said Huck, sadly.

"I want to help poor Muff," said Tom.

"I have a good idea. Let's go to the jail and take him something to eat," said Huck.

Tom and Huck went to the jail with some bread, some apples and a big piece of cold meat. Muff was happy to see them.

"Hello boys!" said Muff, smiling. "No one remembers old Muff anymore, but you're my friends and you remember me. I'm all alone here and there's no one to talk to. Thank you for coming to visit me with this good food."

Tom felt terrible when he left the jail. He thought about poor old Muff and he couldn't sleep at night. He was worried about Muff's trial and he didn't know what to do.

On the day of the trial everyone in St Petersburg was there, even Injun Joe. It was an important trial. Muff looked tired and sad with his old, dirty clothes.

During the trial there were a lot of questions and answers, and things were not going well for Muff. Then the lawyer said, "Call Thomas Sawyer!"

Everyone at the trial turned around and looked at Tom. Why did the lawyer call Tom? What did he know? Tom was nervous and afraid. His heart beat fast and he suddenly felt cold.

The lawyer looked at the young boy and said, "Thomas Sawyer, where were you on June 17 at midnight?"

Tom looked at Injun Joe for a moment and said, "I was in the graveyard."

"Were you near Hoss Williams's grave?" asked the lawyer.

"Yes, sir," answered Tom, nervously.

"Why were you there?" asked the lawyer.

"I went there to see ghosts, with a – a dead cat," said Tom.

Some people at the trial laughed, but the lawyer got angry. He turned around and said, "Silence during the trial, please!"

"What did you see in the graveyard?" asked the lawyer, looking at Tom. "Tell us what happened."

Tom was afraid and spoke very softly.

"Please speak loudly so that everyone can hear you," said the lawyer.

Tom decided to tell the true story, and everyone was amazed.

"…and then Muff Potter fell to the ground and Injun Joe took Muff's knife and –"

Suddenly there was a very loud noise. Injun Joe was jumping out of the window! No one could stop him and he disappeared.

Muff was finally free and he thanked Tom.

Now everyone knew that Injun Joe was the killer. Tom became the hero of St Petersburg because he was brave and he told the truth. His name was in the St Petersburg newspaper and all his friends were proud of him.

"That boy, Tom – he's *really* a good boy," said Aunt Polly, who was especially proud of him. "He told the truth and saved Muff Potter's life."

Tom was happy because he did the right thing. But at night he had terrible dreams about Injun Joe. No one could find him and the sheriff was very angry.

Every young boy wants to find a treasure, and Tom did too. The summer days were long and hot, and Tom wanted an adventure – he wanted to find a treasure. He looked for Joe Harper and Ben Rogers but he couldn't find them anywhere. So he told Huck about his idea.

"That's a great idea!" exclaimed Huck. "Where can we look for a treasure?"

"Well, robbers put treasures under big trees or in old houses," said Tom. "We can start digging under the big tree of Cardiff Hill, near the old house. Come on, Huck! Let's go!"

They climbed up Cardiff Hill under the hot sun and started digging under the big tree. They dug for hours but they didn't find a treasure.

"There's nothing under this tree," said Huck, sitting down. "I'm hot and thirsty."

"Me too," said Tom. "Let's go to the haunted house. No one lives there and haunted houses sometimes have treasures."

"Are you sure haunted houses have treasures?" asked Huck. "I think they have *ghosts*, and I don't want to go inside."

"Ghosts only come out at night and it's daytime now," said Tom, walking towards the haunted house.

"Alright," said Huck, who was afraid of ghosts. "But if I see a ghost I'm going to run away."

CHAPTER 5

The haunted house was a strange place. It was old and scary. There was silence all around. They walked in quietly and looked in all the rooms downstairs. But there was no treasure and there were no ghosts.

They went upstairs and looked around. Tom suddenly said, "Sh!"

"What is it?" whispered Huck. "Do you hear ghosts?"

"No!" whispered Tom. "Don't move! Don't make noise!"

There were holes in the old wooden floor. Through the holes they could see the rooms downstairs.

"Look!" whispered Tom. "There are two men downstairs."

One had long white hair and he was wearing a big hat. He looked like an old Spanish man.

The other man was short and wore dirty clothes.

"Let's listen to them," whispered Tom.

The two men sat on the wooden floor. "It's hot in here and I'm tired," said the old Spanish man.

When the boys heard his voice they were very scared. "It's Injun Joe!" whispered Huck. "It's not a Spanish man, I know his voice." The boys' faces became white. Injun Joe was dressed as an old Spanish man because he didn't want anyone to recognize him.

Injun Joe's friend said, "We have $650 in silver coins. That was a good robbery! What are we going to do with these silver coins?"

"Let's take $30 with us now and hide the bag here," said Injun Joe. "We can come back and get it soon. This is a good hiding place."

The short man moved a big stone in the wall and pulled out a bag. Injun Joe took his knife and started digging in the wall.

Tom and Huck watched with excitement because there was a real treasure downstairs! Six hundred and fifty dollars was a great treasure for two young boys.

Suddenly Injun Joe stopped digging and said, "There's something here. I think it's a box." He found an old black box and opened it slowly.

"Look! It's money!" cried Injun Joe. "There are lots of gold coins inside this box." The two men looked at the coins and put their hands in the box and mixed them. Then they laughed loudly.

The trial

"This was the treasure of the Murrels, who lived here many years ago," said Injun Joe, "and now it's ours!"

"Where can we hide all these coins?" asked the friend. "Can we put them back under the stone?"

"No, no," said Injun Joe, who was thinking. "The stone's not a safe place. Let's put everything under the cross tonight."

When it was dark the two men took the box away. Tom and Huck didn't follow them because they were afraid of Injun Joe. Tom and Huck wanted to find the cross and the big treasure, but *where* was the cross?

THINK!

In this chapter Tom was happy because he did the right thing – he told the truth at the trial. We can see that Tom is growing up and becoming *responsible*. He is no longer only a boy who has adventures and fun. At the trial he has to make an important *decision*: Must he tell the truth or not? He tells the truth even though he is afraid of Injun Joe, and he saves Muff's life. Tom is *honest* and *responsible*.
What does growing up mean to you? Choose one or more answers.

- a ☐ You have more money to spend.
- b ☐ You have more freedom.
- c ☐ You have to make important decisions.
- d ☐ You are responsible for what you do.
- e ☐ You can go on vacation alone.

UNDERSTANDING THE TEXT • page 64
MAPPING VALUES AND FEELINGS • page 78

CHAPTER 6

Inside McDougal's Cave

It was Becky Thatcher's birthday on Saturday and Becky's family and friends were excited. Birthday picnics were always a lot of fun.

One morning Becky met Tom and said, "Tom, you're invited to my birthday picnic near the river. All my friends will be there and we're going to have a big lunch and a chocolate birthday cake. After the picnic we can play games and we can visit McDougal's Cave. Please come!"

Tom liked Becky a lot and said, "Thanks, Becky! It sounds wonderful!" Tom stopped worrying about Injun Joe and the treasure, and thought about Becky's birthday picnic.

On Saturday morning a big boat took Becky, Tom and their friends down the river. There were no mothers and fathers, only a few older boys and girls who were about eighteen years old. It was a beautiful, sunny day and the children had a lot of fun. They played games and

Inside McDougal's Cave

had a big lunch with all kinds of good things to eat and drink. Then everyone sang a birthday song and ate the big chocolate birthday cake.

After the picnic the children went to visit McDougal's Cave. Everyone had candles because it was dark and scary inside the cave. The children played and ran around in the cave, but they always stayed near the entrance. They didn't want to get lost. Tom and Becky wanted to explore the long tunnels of the big cave and they walked and walked until they got lost! They couldn't find the other children.

In the evening the other children got on the boat and went back to St Petersburg. They talked and laughed, but they were very tired. They didn't see that Tom and Becky were not on the boat.

Huck didn't go to the picnic because the mothers in St Petersburg never invited him to birthday picnics. He was alone all day and had time to think about a clever plan. He wanted to find Injun Joe's treasure. He knew that Injun Joe sometimes went to an old house where nobody lived.

That evening he hid behind a tree and watched the old house. It was late and very dark.

He thought, "Injun Joe's in that old house. I'll stay here and wait. When he comes out I'll follow him and I'll find the treasure."

Two men soon came out of the old house. It was Injun Joe and his friend, and Huck followed them quietly. It started raining and the wind started blowing.

"How strange!" thought Huck. "They're going to Widow [1] Douglas's house. But why?"

Suddenly the two men stopped. Injun Joe said, "Many years ago Widow Douglas's husband was very unkind to me. Now I want to hurt his widow. I'm going to cut her face, her nose and her ears. And you have to help me."

Injun Joe's friend looked at him and cried, "No! Please don't hurt the poor old woman!" Injun Joe laughed.

---

1. widow : a woman whose husband is dead.

When Huck heard the conversation he wanted to run away. But then he thought, "Widow Douglas was always kind to me. I must help her. Those bad men are really dangerous."

Huck had an idea and ran to Bill Welsh's house. Bill was a good man and he had two strong sons.

"Mr Welsh, please open! It's me, Huck!"

Mr Welsh opened the door and said, "Huck, what's the matter?"

"Please help me, Mr Welsh," said Huck, "two horrible men want to hurt Widow Douglas!"

Mr Welsh and his sons took their rifles and ran to Widow Douglas's house.

Inside McDougal's Cave

When Injun Joe and his friend saw Mr Welsh and his sons, they ran away and disappeared into the night.

Widow Douglas was frightened and said, "Thank you for helping me. You're all true friends."

Huck went to see Mr Welsh the next day. He was glad because Mr Welsh and his family liked him. Not many people in St Petersburg liked Huck.

"Hello Huck!" said Mr Welsh. "You're a brave boy and you saved Widow Douglas's life. Injun Joe and his friend are dangerous men and we have to find them. Now sit down with my family and have some breakfast."

Huck sat down and looked at the breakfast table with a lot of good things to eat. He smiled and thanked the Welsh family, because they were kind to him.

Huck was happy because he saved Widow Douglas's life. And now he had new friends, the Welsh family.

The next morning all the people in St Petersburg knew that Tom and Becky didn't come back from McDougal's Cave and they were very worried – especially Aunt Polly and Becky's parents. Where were they?

Tom and Becky were lost in McDougal's Cave. They didn't know what to do and they were afraid. Tom took Becky's hand and they walked and walked with their candles. But they couldn't find the entrance of the cave. They were cold and hungry.

At the end of a dark tunnel they found a big empty space with a lot of black bats.

"Oh, no!" cried Becky. "Bats! They're flying everywhere! I'm scared!"

Tom and Becky ran away but the bats followed them. It was terrible! At last the bats went away and Becky started to cry.

CHAPTER 6

"Tom, what are we going to do? We're lost and we'll never find the entrance to the cave."

"Please don't cry, Becky," said Tom softly. "We'll get out of this cave, you'll see."

"No one will ever find us," said Becky. "There are too many long tunnels… we're going to die here."

"Don't worry," said Tom bravely. "I'll find the way out of this cave!"

They ate their last piece of cake. Suddenly their last candle went out – now it was dark inside the cave. What time was it? What day was it? They didn't know and they fell asleep.

When they woke up they were hungry and thirsty. Tom heard a noise.

"Becky!" said Tom. "Did you hear a noise? Someone is looking for us!"

Becky looked at Tom and smiled.

"You stay here, and I'm going to see. Don't move!" said Tom.

"I'll wait here," said Becky.

 THINK!

In St Petersburg all the people know each other. It's a small community. Huck knows Widow Douglas and he remembers her kindness. When she's in danger he runs to Mr Welsh for help. Mr Welsh and his sons immediately take their rifles and go and help Widow Douglas. Huck makes new friends. When Tom and Becky don't come back from the birthday picnic everyone in town is worried. People *care* about each other and *help* each other.
Things are very different in a big city, where most people don't know each other. Which do you prefer, a small community or a big city? Say why.

UNDERSTANDING THE TEXT • page 66
MAPPING VALUES AND FEELINGS • page 78

CHAPTER 7

The treasure box

Tom went into the dark tunnel slowly. He saw a light and heard a noise.

"Someone is looking for us, but *who*?" Tom thought.

Then he saw a big hand with a candle – it was Injun Joe! Tom was terribly frightened and didn't move.

"Why is Injun Joe here?" he thought. "Is he looking for me?"

Since it was very dark in the cave Injun Joe didn't see Tom. Suddenly he went away and Tom went back to Becky, who was happy to see him. Tom didn't tell her about Injun Joe because she wasn't feeling well.

It was Tuesday and everyone in St Petersburg was worried about Becky and Tom.

"Where *are* Becky and Tom?" asked an old woman.

"They're lost in the cave," said a young man.

"We have to go and look for them," said the sheriff. "Let's all go together!"

CHAPTER 7

A lot of people from the town went to the cave in the morning and looked for them. But at the end of the day no one could find them. Mrs Thatcher was very worried and became ill. Aunt Polly couldn't sleep at night and her hair became whiter than before. She, too, was very worried and upset.

Then on Tuesday night there was a lot of noise and excitement in the streets of St Petersburg.

"Look! They're here! Becky and Tom are here!" shouted the people happily.

"We were so worried about them," said one young girl.

"That cave's dangerous," said an old man. "If you get lost there, it's almost impossible to find your way out."

"Becky and Tom were very lucky," said an old woman, smiling.

No one went to sleep that night. Everyone listened to Tom's exciting story about his adventure in the cave.

"Becky and I were lost for a long time," he said. "We were scared and hungry. Suddenly I remembered the string[1] in my pocket. I used the long string to help me. I went down many tunnels, and I always returned to Becky because I followed the string. Then I found another entrance to the cave. It was a very small entrance and it was near the river."

"Hurrah for Tom and Becky!" everyone shouted happily.

Tom and Becky were happy because they were home, but they were tired and hungry. Becky was very weak and she stayed in bed for many days. And Tom wasn't feeling well either, so he stayed in bed for a few days too.

A few weeks after Becky's birthday picnic Tom went to visit her at home. Becky was pleased to see her friend Tom and they talked about their scary adventure in the cave.

Becky's father, Mr Thatcher, asked Tom, "Do you want to go to the cave again?"

"I'm not afraid of the cave," said Tom bravely.

---

1. string :

The treasure box

"Well, no one is going into that cave again," said Mr Thatcher. "It's a dangerous place. There are two big doors in front of the entrance now. And I have the keys."

"Oh, no!" cried Tom and his face became white.

"What's wrong, Tom?" asked Mr Thatcher.

"Injun Joe's inside the cave!" exclaimed Tom.

"What!" cried Mr Thatcher. "We must go to the cave immediately!"

Mr Thatcher and the other men from St Petersburg went to the cave and opened the big doors. They looked around and found Injun Joe on the ground – he was dead.

After Injun Joe's funeral Tom went to see Huck.

"Now that Injun Joe's dead we'll never find the money," said Huck sadly.

"No, Huck!" said Tom excitedly. "I know where the money is!"

"Really?" asked Huck, who couldn't believe his ears. "Where is it?"

"It's inside the cave," said Tom. "I saw Injun Joe in the cave. He hid the money there."

"That's great, Tom!" cried Huck.

"We can find it easily," said Tom, smiling.

"But how?" asked Huck. "It's a big, dark cave and we'll get lost inside. And now there are two big doors at the entrance."

"We won't get lost in the cave," said Tom, "because I have candles and a long string. And I'll bring a spade, too."

"Good!" cried Huck. "Let's go and get a boat."

They took a small boat and went down the Mississippi River to McDougal's Cave.

"Here's the other entrance," said Tom, showing Huck a small entrance near the river.

"What a small entrance!" said Huck. "That's why nobody knows about it."

Tom and Huck went into the cave. They were careful and used the candles and the long string to help them.

They walked in the long tunnels and Tom suddenly stopped.

"This is where I saw Injun Joe," said Tom.

"His ghost is probably here too," said Huck, who was afraid of ghosts.

"Oh, don't worry about ghosts," said Tom. "We have to find the hiding place."

"Alright," said Huck, looking around. "Remember, Injun Joe said 'we'll hide it under the cross.'"

"Let's look for the cross," said Tom. "Hmm… Injun Joe was standing here."

The two boys looked everywhere and suddenly Tom cried, "Here's the cross!" There was a big black cross on the wall of the cave.

"We found it!" said Huck happily.

"Now let's start to dig *under* the cross," said Tom, taking the spade.

The treasure box

They dug and dug, and found some wooden boards [2].

"Let's move these heavy wooden boards," said Huck. "There's probably something under them."

They found a small room with a bed, some old candles and a few bottles.

"Look, near the bed… it's the treasure box!" cried Tom.

"Let's open it and see what's inside!" cried Huck.

They opened the old treasure box and found a lot of gold and silver coins. They couldn't believe their eyes.

"We're rich… rich!" cried Huck happily.

"This is wonderful!" exclaimed Tom, looking at all the coins. The boys put their hands in the treasure box and touched the gold and silver coins.

"Now let's take our treasure and get out of this cave!" said Tom.

They took the old treasure box and followed the long string to the small entrance of the cave. They got into the boat and went up the river. When they got to St Petersburg Tom said, "Let's take the treasure to Aunt Polly's house."

A lot of people in St Petersburg saw the two boys and the old treasure box. They followed them to Aunt Polly's house because they were very curious [3].

Aunt Polly was surprised to see Tom and Huck and all the people.

"Tom, Huck, what are you doing?" she asked. "What's in that old box?"

Tom and Huck put the treasure box on the kitchen table.

"It's a big surprise, Aunt Polly!" said Tom, slowly opening the treasure box.

---

2. **wooden board** : big, flat piece of wood.
3. **curious** : (here) when you want to know more about something.

CHAPTER 7

Everyone was amazed and looked at all the silver and gold coins. Tom and Huck counted the coins and everyone watched in silence.

"We have $12,000!" cried Tom and Huck. "$12,000! We're rich!"

There were $12,000!

Aunt Polly was very surprised and she couldn't say a word. Tom told his long story about Injun Joe and the treasure in McDougal's Cave. It was an exciting story and the people of St Petersburg listened with great interest.

"Half of the treasure is Huck's and half is mine!" said Tom, smiling at his friend.

The town newspaper wrote a long article about their adventure. Tom and Huck were now the richest and most famous people in town. Everyone was proud of them and looked at them kindly.

They were the heroes [4] of St Petersburg.

---

4. **hero** : someone who does something brave or good.

THINK!

Read this sentence taken from this chapter.

Tom and Huck were now the richest and most famous people in town. Everyone was proud of them and looked at them kindly.

Tom and Huck are now rich and famous, and everyone likes them. The people of St Petersburg now like Huck, but they didn't like him before. Why do you think they suddenly like Huck? Choose one or more answers.

- a ☐ Because he's brave.
- b ☐ Because he's rich.
- c ☐ Because he helped Widow Douglas.
- d ☐ Because he's clever.
- e ☐ Because he's honest.

UNDERSTANDING THE TEXT • page 68

MAPPING VALUES AND FEELINGS • page 78

Missouri: the door to the West

The city of Independence, Missouri is often called "the door to the West". In the 1840s thousands of pioneers began their long trip to the West in Independence. These people came from different states east of the Mississippi River and they wanted to go and live in the West. At Independence the settlers had to decide where they wanted to go. They had to choose a trail: [1] the Oregon Trail, the California Trail or the Santa Fe Trail.

At that time the United States Government often gave free land to pioneers who wanted to set up farms and towns in the West. Pioneers were strong, brave people. These people met in Independence with their covered wagons [2] pulled by horses. Families put their furniture, clothes, food, water and other useful things in the covered wagons. Many families brought cattle [3] with them because they wanted to start a cattle farm.

1. **trail :** (here) a new, long path across America.
2. **covered wagon :**
3. **cattle :**

The pioneers met in Independence early in the spring. Many covered wagons always traveled together because it was safer. This was called a wagon train and every wagon train had a leader called a captain. There was always a scout, too, who knew the trails well. He rode his horse in front of the wagon train to look for dangers.

The long trip to the West took many months, and it was difficult and dangerous. It was difficult to cross big rivers and climb tall mountains. The weather was another problem. In the summer it was very hot and there was little water to drink. There was little grass for the animals to eat. In other seasons, heavy rain and snow were also a big problem.

Look at a typical day on the trail:

5 am
The pioneers got up and had breakfast. Then they began to travel.

Noon
The pioneers and the animals rested and had something to eat.

2 pm
The wagon trains began to travel again.

Sunset
At sunset the scout chose a safe place to stop for the night. The wagon train made a big circle to protect everyone from wild animals and possible American Indian attacks. The pioneers sat around the fire and had dinner and talked. They went to sleep early because they were tired. A day on the trail wasn't easy!

Between 1841 and 1869 more than 500,000 pioneers traveled from Independence, Missouri to the West. These people set up farms, towns, roads, cities and industries – they built America.

COMPREHENSION CHECK

1. Choose the correct answer.

1. The pioneers came from states *west / east* of the Mississippi River.
2. The pioneers could choose one of *three / two* trails.
3. The pioneers were *rich / brave* people.
4. The United States Government gave free *land / cattle* to settlers who went to the *West / East*.
5. The leader of a wagon train was called a *scout / captain*.
6. The wagon trains started to travel early in the *summer / spring*.
7. The trip to the West took *a year / many months*.

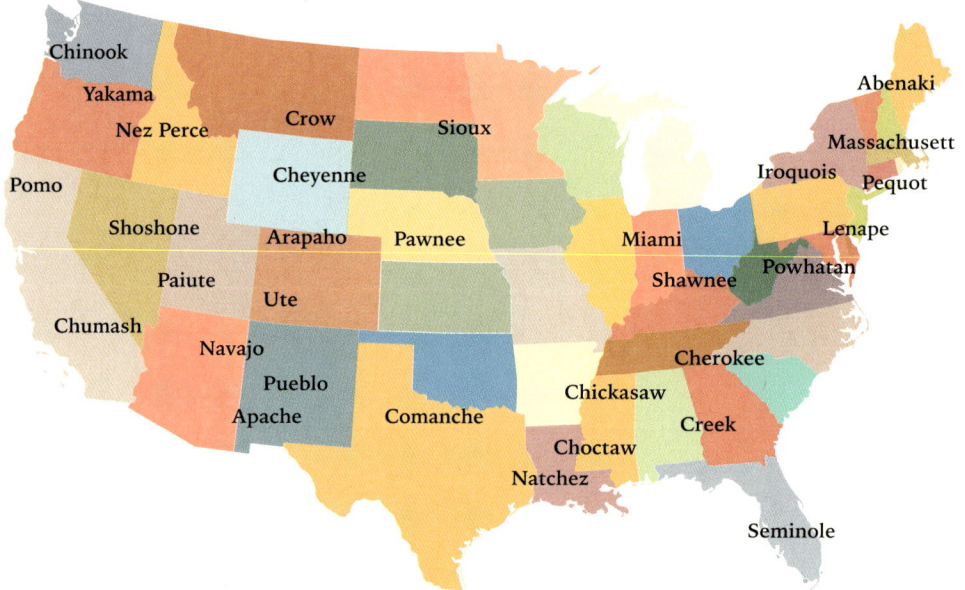

Native American Indians

The first Americans

American Indians came from Asia about 13,000 years ago. They crossed the Bering Strait and then they slowly went down to North and South America. These people lived in many different tribes [1] all over North America and every tribe had a leader, called a chief. Some of these tribes were the Sioux, the Cherokee, the Apache, the Comanche and the Navajo.

American Indians were strong and healthy, and lived outdoors most of the time. They loved nature and respected it, because it often had an important religious meaning.

When the first European explorers arrived in North America in the 1500s, about 20 million American Indians lived there. The explorers brought horses and guns, and they began to explore the new continent. In the late 1700s many Indians began to die from the illnesses that the explorers brought to the new world.

1. **tribe :** (here) a group of American Indians that live together.

The Indian Wars

In the late 1700s thousands of Europeans settlers [2] began to travel West of the Appalachian Mountains. They took the land from the Indians. In the early 1800s thousands of settlers moved across North America in covered wagons. [3] The American Indians were very angry and in the 1830s the Indian Wars started.

They attacked the settlers and the United States Army. The American Indians were great warriors and fought bravely. The Indian Wars continued until about 1890, when the American Indians lost all of their lands. Today we still remember the names of some great chiefs and warriors: Geronimo and Cochise of the Apache tribe, Sitting Bull and Crazy Horse of the Lakota Sioux tribe, and Chief Joseph of the Nez Perce tribe.

The Battle of Little Big Horn, June 25th 1876.

2. **settlers** : people who go and live in a new place.

3. **covered wagon :**

In 1869 the first American transcontinental railroad was built and the West became easy to reach for everyone. No one could stop the settlers now.
By the end of the 19th century the American Indians lost their land, their homes and their way of life. This was a very sad period in American history. The American Indians had to go and live on government reservations,[4] and life there was not easy or pleasant.

American Indians today

Today there are about 5.2 million American Indians living in the United States, and about 1.2 million live on one of the 275 reservations.
American Indians are proud of their history, language and traditions. Every year there are more than a thousand pow-wows in the United States. Pow-wows are big meetings of different tribes where there is music, dancing and other events.
The American TV series "500 Nations" (1995), starring Kevin Costner, explored the long and interesting history of the American Indian nations of North America. The series was very successful because people wanted to know more about the American Indian tribes.

---

4. **reservation**: (here) government land where the American Indians had to live.

COMPREHENSION CHECK

1. Are the following sentences true (T) or false (F)? Correct the false ones.

	T	F
1. The American Indians came from South America.	☐	☐
2. The leader of a tribe was called a chief.	☐	☐
3. When the first European explorers arrived in North America, about 20,000 American Indians lived there.	☐	☐
4. The settlers took the land away from the American Indians.	☐	☐
5. The Indian Wars started in the 1700s.	☐	☐
6. After 1869 many settlers traveled to the West on the train.	☐	☐
7. Today some American Indians still live on government reservations.	☐	☐
8. A "pow-wow" is an old Indian dance.	☐	☐

ACTIVITIES

Understanding the text

Chapter 1	56
Chapter 2	58
Chapter 3	60
Chapter 4	62
Chapter 5	64
Chapter 6	66
Chapter 7	68

Extra listening — 70

Surf the net — 72

Trinity • Preparation — 73

Key • Preparation — 74

Exit test • Let's revise the story — 76

Values & Feelings — 78

CHAPTER 1 UNDERSTANDING THE TEXT

1. COMPREHENSION CHECK • For each sentence, choose true (T), false (F), or doesn't say (D). There is an example at the beginning (0).

		T	F	D
0.	Aunt Polly found Tom under the bed with the cat.	☐	☒	☐
1.	Aunt Polly had white hair and wore glasses.	☐	☐	☐
2.	Tom Sawyer was a tall boy of twelve.	☐	☐	☐
3.	During the summer evenings, Tom liked walking in St Petersburg.	☐	☐	☐
4.	The big boy came from New York City.	☐	☐	☐
5.	Tom and the big boy became good friends.	☐	☐	☐
6.	On Saturday morning Tom had to paint the big fence.	☐	☐	☐
7.	Tom told Ben Rogers that he liked painting the big fence.	☐	☐	☐
8.	Ben Rogers gave Tom a new kite because he wanted to paint the fence.	☐	☐	☐
9.	Aunt Polly gave Tom a red apple because he painted the fence well.	☐	☐	☐

2. VOCABULARY • Odd one out! Circle the word in each group which is different from the others and say why.

1.	cat	dog	rat	fish
2.	jacket	shoes	shirt	tie
3.	jam	apple	orange	banana
4.	kitchen	bedroom	garden	bathroom
5.	summer	season	spring	winter

3. VOCABULARY • Use the odd words to complete the sentences.

1. Summer was Tom's favorite …………………… .
2. Aunt Polly cooked …………………… for dinner.
3. Aunt Polly had a lot of flowers in her …………………… .
4. Tom didn't wear any …………………… on his feet.
5. Tom liked eating …………………… .

UNDERSTANDING THE TEXT

4. WORD SQUARE • Find the seven things that Tom's friends gave him and circle them.

```
N M A E I O U Z P H J U N S
I H S D C A T B H O T S C R
C V B G A Z G U C B K J R U
K A S O C E A I M G D I A O
F P B R T U C L E M E N T F
O P D V F T D D T P H O S E
A L G P N I L O A G K E Y T
C E R G V J F E Y C A H V M
X T S D W P J G X V R A B N
R E O X K N I F E T B N E S
O Z Y B T Y O E S R E A P H
```

5. VOCABULARY • Now complete the sentences with the seven words you found.

1. The girls were afraid of the dead ....
2. Tom went to fly his .... on a windy day.
3. Aunt Polly's old .... couldn't see well because he had only one eye.
4. The boys drank a .... of water because they were thirsty.
5. There was a big, red .... on the tree.
6. Aunt Polly opened the door of her house with a ....
7. "I need a .... to cut the apple," said Tom.

6. READING PICTURES • Look at the picture on page 13 and answer these questions.

1. What is Tom standing on and why?
2. What is Tom holding in his hands?
3. What is Ben Rogers saying to Tom?
4. What is Tom thinking?

CHAPTER 2 UNDERSTANDING THE TEXT

1. COMPREHENSION CHECK • Read these sentences about Chapter Two. Choose the correct answer – a, b or c. There is an example at the beginning (0).

0. Tom didn't like his Sunday clothes
- a ☐ because they were old.
- b ✗ because they were uncomfortable.
- c ☐ so he didn't wear them.

1. When Tom was in church
- a ☐ he was always happy.
- b ☐ he was always hungry.
- c ☐ he was always bored.

2. On Sunday Tom brought
- a ☐ a black beetle to church.
- b ☐ a little dog to church.
- c ☐ a dead cat to church.

3. The children of St Petersburg
- a ☐ always played with Huck Finn.
- b ☐ didn't talk to Huck Finn.
- c ☐ liked Huck Finn a lot.

4. Tom and Huck decided
- a ☐ to go fishing together in the morning.
- b ☐ to go to the graveyard together at night.
- c ☐ to go and talk to Mrs Hopkins after school.

5. Huck said that
- a ☐ Hoss was the name of a dead cat.
- b ☐ a dead cat could call ghosts out of their graves.
- c ☐ Mrs Hopkins gave him a dead cat.

6. Tom got dressed and went out of the bedroom window at
- a ☐ midnight.
- b ☐ ten o'clock.
- c ☐ eleven o'clock.

UNDERSTANDING THE TEXT

COMPARATIVE ADJECTIVES

*"It's **easier than** you think,"* said Huck.

Easier is a comparative adjective. We form comparative adjectives like this:

- if the adjective has one syllable, we add **-er**:

    tall – tall**er**   old – old**er**

- if the adjective is short and ends with a vowel + consonant, like "big", we double the final consonant:

    big – bi**gg**er   hot – ho**tt**er

- if the adjective has two syllables and ends with **-y**, we change the **-y** to **-i** and add **-er**:

    easy – eas**ier**   happy – happ**ier**

- if the adjective has two or more syllables, we use **more** before the adjective:

    difficult – **more** difficult   interesting – **more** interesting

Be careful! Some adjectives have an **irregular comparative** form:

good – **better**   bad – **worse**   far – **farther/further**

2. GRAMMAR • Fill in the gaps with the correct comparative adjective.

1. Sid is .... than his brother, Tom. (*short*)
2. Swimming is .... than going to school. (*exciting*)
3. Mary Harper is pretty, but Becky Thatcher is .... (*pretty*)
4. Aunt Polly is .... than Mrs Hopkins. (*old*)
5. New York City is .... than St Petersburg. (*interesting*)
6. Huck Finn can run .... than Tom. (*fast*)
7. The English test was .... than the history test. (*easy*)
8. Becky's house is .... than Tom's house. (*big*)
9. The month of August is .... than the month of May in the USA. (*hot*)
10. Becky is a .... student than Tom. (*good*)

CHAPTER 3 UNDERSTANDING THE TEXT

1. COMPREHENSION CHECK • Match the following sentences (1-10) with the endings (a-j).

1. ☐ Huck was frightened
2. ☐ Tom and Huck hid
3. ☐ Suddenly the two boys saw
4. ☐ The grave robbers wanted
5. ☐ Huck's father told him
6. ☐ Muff Potter asked Doctor Robinson
7. ☐ Doctor Robinson got angry with Muff Potter
8. ☐ Doctor Robinson hit Muff on the head
9. ☐ Muff Potter didn't remember what happened
10. ☐ Tom and Huck saw everything that happened

a that the ghosts were real people.
b for more money.
c and Injun Joe took Muff's knife and killed the doctor.
d when he saw ghosts at the graveyard.
e and he thought he killed Doctor Robinson.
f to steal a dead body for Doctor Robinson.
g and they ran away because they were scared.
h behind a big tree.
i and the two men started to fight.
j about Doctor Robinson.

2. VOCABULARY • Read the descriptions below and then write the correct word for each one. The first letter is already there. There is one space for each other letter in the word. There is an example at the beginning.

0. To make a hole in the ground: d _i g_
1. A person who steals things from other people: r _ _ _ _ _
2. You use it to cut things: k _ _ _ _
3. Little games, jokes: t _ _ _ _ _
4. Afraid, frightened: s _ _ _ _ _

UNDERSTANDING THE TEXT

3. GRAMMAR • Complete sentences 1-10 with the prepositions in the box below.

> in • outside • for • inside • with • on •
> near • under • behind • at

1. They opened the box and looked ....
2. Tom sat .... a big tree and ate an apple.
3. The boys played .... the ball all afternoon.
4. "This picture is .... you, Becky," said Tom.
5. There were ten children .... Tom's class.
6. "Come and call me .... eleven o'clock," said Tom.
7. "You must go to school .... Monday!" said Aunt Polly.
8. Tom and Huck hid .... a big tree at the graveyard.
9. Tom was happy because he could sit .... Becky Thatcher.
10. Huck waited for Tom .... in the garden.

4. WRITING • You are Tom and you keep a diary. Complete your diary and write the correct word in each space. The first is already there.

I had (0) ....*a*.... very scary evening. I went (1) .... the graveyard with Huck. He brought a dead (2) .... in a big bag. We saw (3) .... men who were grave robbers. They wanted (4) .... steal a dead (5) .... Then they started to (6) .... Injun Joe (7) .... Dr Robinson with Muff Potter's (8) .... It was terrible! Huck (9) .... I ran away because (10) .... were frightened. We hid in an old (11) .... near the river.

5. READING PICTURES • Look at the picture on page 23 and answer these questions.

1. What is Injun Joe holding in his right hand?
2. Who is Injun Joe looking at and what is he thinking?
3. Describe the graveyard.

CHAPTER 4 UNDERSTANDING THE TEXT

1. COMPREHENSION CHECK • Read the summary of Chapter Four and choose the best word – a, b or c – for each space. There is an example at the beginning.

The people in St Petersburg soon found (**0**) ….*c*…. about Doctor Robinson, and (**1**) ……… sheriff put Muff Potter in jail. Tom and Huck (**2**) ……… that Injun Joe killed Doctor Robinson, (**3**) ……… they couldn't tell (**4**) ……… . They were really afraid of Injun Joe. Tom couldn't forget the terrible night at the graveyard and he was very sad. Aunt Polly was (**5**) ……… about him.

Tom, Joe Harper and Huck (**6**) ……… to go and live on Jackson's Island and have fun. Tom and Joe Harper did not tell (**7**) ……… families. One day they saw a big steamboat with (**8**) ……… of people. They were looking for a dead body in the river. Tom (**9**) ……… , "They're looking for (**10**) ……… !" The boys laughed.

That night he went back to St Petersburg and returned to Jackson's Island the next morning. He explained (**11**) ……… to Joe and Huck, and he had an idea. They went back to St Petersburg and walked into the church (**12**) ……… their own funeral! Everyone was very surprised and happy to see (**13**) ……… .

	a	b	c
0.	on	in	(out)
1.	a	the	he
2.	knew	understood	learned
3.	so	but	why
4.	anyone	no one	nobody
5.	nervous	worried	sad
6.	decided	decision	deciding
7.	them	their	his
8.	much	many	a lot
9.	said	told	spoke
10.	we	us	he
11.	everyone	everywhere	everything
12.	during	in	by
13.	they	those	them

UNDERSTANDING THE TEXT

SUPERLATIVES

*"This is **the best** breakfast in the world!" exclaimed Huck, who was always hungry.*

Best is a superlative adjective. We form the superlative of adjectives like this:
- if the adjective has one syllable, we add **-est**:

  *cold – **the** cold**est**   tall – **the** tall**est**   old – **the** old**est***
- if the adjective is short and ends with a vowel + consonant, like "big", we double the final consonant:

  *big – **the** big**gest**   hot – **the** hot**test***
- if the adjective has two syllables and ends with **-y**, we change the **-y** to **-i** and add **-est**:

  *hungry – **the** hungr**iest**   pretty – **the** prett**iest**   happy – **the** happ**iest***
- if the adjective has two or more syllables, we use **most** before the adjective:

  *interesting – **the most** interesting   modern – **the most** modern*

Be careful! Some adjectives have an **irregular superlative** form:

*good – **the best**   bad – **the worst**   far – **the farthest/furthest***

We generally use the preposition ***in*** after a superlative:

*It's the longest river **in** America. It was the hottest day **in** the summer.*

2. GRAMMAR • Fill in the gaps with the correct superlative adjective.

1. Mary is the .... girl in Joe's class. (*nice*)
2. Mark Twain was the .... writer in the Gold Country. (*famous*)
3. The Mississippi River is the .... river in the United States. (*big*)
4. Aunt Polly's fence was the .... in town. (*long*)
5. Becky was the .... girl in school. (*pretty*)
6. Aunt Polly made the .... jam in St Petersburg. (*good*)
7. Injun Joe was the .... man in town. (*dangerous*)
8. Ben Rogers was the .... student in Tom's class. (*bad*)
9. Winter is the .... season of the year in Missouri. (*cold*)
10. Becky Thatcher's father was the .... man in town. (*tall*)

CHAPTER 5 UNDERSTANDING THE TEXT

1. COMPREHENSION CHECK • For each sentence, choose true (T), false (F), or doesn't say (D). There is an example at the beginning (0).

		T	F	D
0.	Tom met Huck at Cardiff Hill.	☒	☐	☐
1.	Tom and Huck went to visit Muff in jail and brought him some food.	☐	☐	☐
2.	At the trial Tom did not answer the lawyer's questions.	☐	☐	☐
3.	The lawyer got angry because some people laughed during the trial.	☐	☐	☐
4.	During the trial Injun Joe ran out of the front door.	☐	☐	☐
5.	Huck didn't want to go inside the haunted house because he was afraid of ghosts.	☐	☐	☐
6.	Tom and Huck heard the voices of the two men and one of them was Injun Joe.	☐	☐	☐
7.	Injun Joe's friend was a short man called Jack.	☐	☐	☐
8.	Injun Joe found an old black box with a treasure under a big tree.	☐	☐	☐
9.	The treasure belonged to the Murrels.	☐	☐	☐
10.	Injun Joe decided to hide the treasure under the cross.	☐	☐	☐

2. VOCABULARY • Read the descriptions below and write the correct word for each one. The first letter is already there. There is one space for each other letter in the word. There is an example at the beginning.

0. a religious person in the church: r _e v e r e n d_
1. a ceremony when a person dies: f _ _ _ _ _ _
2. happy and satisfied: p _ _ _ _
3. a person who advises people on legal problems: l _ _ _ _ _
4. when you know who someone is when you see them: r _ _ _ _ _ _ _ _
5. when you speak very softly: w _ _ _ _ _ _
6. Muff was put here: j _ _ _
7. a precious metal used to make coins : g _ _ _
8. a black insect : b _ _ _ _ _
9. a person who kills someone : k _ _ _ _ _

UNDERSTANDING THE TEXT

THE PAST SIMPLE

*Muff **looked** tired and sad with his old, dirty clothes.*
*When it **was** dark the two men **took** the box away.*

We form the Past Simple of regular verbs by adding **-ed** to the verb:
 talk – talk**ed**   work – work**ed**   help – help**ed**

When the verb already ends in **-e**, add only **-d** to the verb:
 like – like**d**   love – love**d**   complete – complete**d**

Some verbs end in a consonant **+ y**. We change the **-y** to **-i** and add **-ed**:
 carry – carr**ied**   study – stud**ied**   hurry – hurr**ied**

But if verbs end in a vowel **+ y**, the "y" does not change:
 play – play**ed**   stay – stay**ed**   enjoy – enjoy**ed**

Irregular verbs

Some verbs have irregular Past Simple forms, e.g. **was** (be) and **took** (take).

Verb	Past Simple	Verb	Past Simple
buy	bought	leave	left
go	went	think	thought
know	knew	write	wrote

3. GRAMMAR • Complete the following sentences with the Past Simple of the verbs in the box.

> hit • swim • carry • paint • cook • cry • get • say • drink • kill

1. Aunt Polly .... dinner at six o'clock.
2. Huck .... a dead cat in a big bag.
3. Tom was a good swimmer and he .... all the way to Jackson's Island.
4. The teacher .... , "Silence in the classroom!"
5. Tom .... a big glass of milk at breakfast.
6. Everyone in church .... during the funeral.
7. "Muff, you .... Doctor Robinson!" Injun Joe said.
8. On Monday morning Tom .... up early because he had to go to school.
9. The big boy .... Tom on the nose.
10. Tom and his friends .... the big fence.

CHAPTER 6 UNDERSTANDING THE TEXT

1. COMPREHENSION CHECK • Are these sentences true (T) or false (F)?

		T	F
0.	Becky Thatcher invited all her friends to her birthday picnic.	☒	☐
1.	Becky's birthday picnic was in the garden of her home.	☐	☐
2.	There were no parents at the birthday picnic.	☐	☐
3.	The children visited McDougal's Cave and they all had candles because it was very dark inside the cave.	☐	☐
4.	Tom and Becky got lost because they lost their candles.	☐	☐
5.	Huck Finn did not go to Becky's birthday picnic.	☐	☐
6.	Injun Joe and his friend hid the treasure in Widow Douglas's house.	☐	☐
7.	Mr Welsh and his sons took their rifles and ran to Widow Douglas's house.	☐	☐
8.	Mr Welsh invited Huck to dinner at his house.	☐	☐
9.	Becky and Tom were frightened because they were lost in McDougal's Cave.	☐	☐
10.	Tom heard a noise in the cave and went to see what it was.	☐	☐

2. CHARACTERS • Look at the pictures of the characters below. Can you describe them? Use the words in the box to write some sentences about each one.

> liked adventures • old • wore glasses • got bored in church • never went to school • was always happy • liked to go fishing • had white hair • kind • bad • a killer • wore old clothes • didn't wear shoes • clever • liked to go swimming • didn't like to work • brave • dangerous • pretty • blue eyes • blonde hair • friendly • an American Indian • a robber

....
....

UNDERSTANDING THE TEXT

3. WRITING • You are Huck. Complete your diary with the words in the box. There is an example at the beginning.

> picnic • danger • treasure • tree • rifles • inside • them • friends • alone • two • plan • sons • hurt • me

Today was Becky's birthday (**0**) …*picnic*… but I didn't go. No one invited (**1**) ……………. .

I was (**2**) …………… all day and I thought about a clever (**3**) …………… to find Injun Joe's (**4**) …………… .

I hid behind a big (**5**) …………… and watched an old house. I knew that Injun Joe was (**6**) …………… that old house.

When (**7**) …………… men came out of the house I followed (**8**) …………… . They went to Widow Douglas's house and they wanted to (**9**) …………… her.

I ran to Bill Welsh's house. I told him that Widow Douglas was in (**10**) …………… . Bill and his (**11**) …………… took their (**12**) …………… and went to Widow Douglas's house. When Injun Joe and his friend saw them, they ran away.

Now Bill Welsh and his family are my new (**13**) …………… and I'm very happy.

4. SPEAKING • Tom and Becky are afraid of bats. Work with your partner and talk about the animals you are afraid of and say why. Make a list of these animals and compare it with your classmates.

5. READING PICS • Look at the picture on page 40 and answer these questions.

1. What are the three men doing?
2. What are the three men carrying?
3. What is Huck saying to them?
4. How do the three men feel?

CHAPTER 7 UNDERSTANDING THE TEXT

1. COMPREHENSION CHECK • Read these sentences about Chapter Seven. Choose the correct answer – a, b or c. There is an example at the beginning (0).

0. Tom was terribly frightened
   - a ☒ because he thought Injun Joe was looking for him.
   - b ☐ because his candle went out.
   - c ☐ because he hated bats.

1. The people of St Petersburg were worried
   - a ☐ because Mrs Thatcher became ill.
   - b ☐ because Injun Joe disappeared.
   - c ☐ because Tom and Becky were lost.

2. Tom and Becky were able to get out of the cave
   - a ☐ because Tom used a long string.
   - b ☐ because the people of St Petersburg went into the cave and found them.
   - c ☐ because Mr Thatcher helped them.

3. Mr Thatcher had the keys
   - a ☐ to the treasure box of the Murrel family.
   - b ☐ to Widow Douglas's house.
   - c ☐ to the big doors at the entrance of McDougal's Cave.

4. Tom and Huck went back to McDougal's Cave
   - a ☐ but they used the small entrance near the river.
   - b ☐ to look for Injun Joe.
   - c ☐ and they both got lost.

5. Tom and Huck started to dig under the black cross
   - a ☐ and they found Injun Joe's dead body.
   - b ☐ and they found an empty box.
   - c ☐ and they found the treasure.

6. The people of St Petersburg followed Tom and Huck
   - a ☐ because they were curious.
   - b ☐ because they wanted part of the treasure.
   - c ☐ because they wanted to listen to Tom's story.

UNDERSTANDING THE TEXT

2. CROSSWORD PUZZLE

ACROSS

1. Aunt Polly makes this.
4.
6.
7.
9.
11. Tom and Huck live near this big river.

DOWN

2.
3. Tom and Huck live in this American state.
5. long, dark path underground
8. when you want to know more about something
10. this woman's husband is dead
12.

EXTRA LISTENING

1. Listen to Tom's teacher tell the story of the Lewis and Clark Expedition. Then choose the correct answer – a, b or c.

1. When did President Thomas Jefferson buy the Louisiana Purchase?

a ☐

b ☐

c ☐

2. How much did President Thomas Jefferson pay for the Louisiana Purchase?

a ☐

b ☐

c ☐

3. How did the Lewis and Clark expedition travel up the Missouri River?

a ☐

b ☐

c ☐

4. Who was Sacagawea?

a ☐

b ☐

c ☐

5. What did Sacagawea's brother give the Lewis and Clark expedition?

a ☐

b ☐

c ☐

EXTRA LISTENING

2. Listen to the recording and then choose the correct answer – a, b or c.

1. When did the school day begin?
   - a ☐ at four o'clock
   - b ☐ at eight o'clock
   - c ☐ at nine o'clock
2. What was the second subject of the day?
   - a ☐ Math
   - b ☐ Geography
   - c ☐ Reading
3. What did students do when they got home after school?
   - a ☐ They worked on the family farm.
   - b ☐ They did their homework.
   - c ☐ They played.
4. Who cleaned the classroom after school?
   - a ☐ the parents of the students
   - b ☐ the students
   - c ☐ the teacher
5. How many rooms were in the school?
   - a ☐ three
   - b ☐ two
   - c ☐ one
6. What was behind the teacher's desk?
   - a ☐ a big blackboard
   - b ☐ an American flag
   - c ☐ a big bell

SURF THE NET

Let's find out more about bats!

Work with a partner and surf the net. Look for information on bats and answer these questions. Then present your work to the class.

1. Are bats birds or mammals? Why?
2. Why are bats called night animals?
3. How many different kinds of bats are there in the world? Name three different kinds.
4. What food do bats eat?
5. What is the name of the smallest bat?
6. What is the name of the biggest bat?
7. Where do bats usually live?
8. Why are bats important in Nature?

TRINITY • PREPARATION

1. GRADE 3 – FREE TIME • Tom and Huck go fishing in their free time. Use these questions to talk to the class about what you do in your free time.

1. What are three things you do in your free time?
2. Are they easy, difficult or dangerous to do?
3. Who do you do them with?
4. Why do you like them?

2. GRADE 3 – JOBS • Doctor Robinson was a doctor. Talk with your partner about the job you want to do. Use these questions to help you.

1. What kind of job do you want to do?
2. Why do you want to do this job?
3. Is it easy, difficult, interesting or dangerous?
4. What subjects do you need to study to do this job?
5. Do you know someone who does this job?

3. GRADE 4 – FOOD • There was a lot of good food at Becky's birthday picnic. Talk about food with your partner and use these questions to help you.

1. What is your favorite food?
2. Where do you eat it?
3. What food do you hate?
4. Who cooks at your house?
5. Do you like food from other countries?

KEY • PREPARATION

1. READING AND WRITING PART 3 • Complete the conversations (1-4) with the correct answer – a, b or c. There is an example at the beginning (0).

0. Pass me the butter.
- a ☐ You're welcome.
- b ☒ Here you are.
- c ☐ Thank you.

1. What time does the library open?
- a ☐ It's late.
- b ☐ Not now.
- c ☐ I don't know.

2. I'll meet you at two o'clock.
- a ☐ Yes, I am.
- b ☐ Yes, I do.
- c ☐ Please be on time.

3. Are the boys ready?
- a ☐ Almost.
- b ☐ Already.
- c ☐ Quite.

4. Can you come swimming with me?
- a ☐ No, I don't.
- b ☐ No, I can't.
- c ☐ No, I'm not.

2. READING AND WRITING PART 7 • You are Tom. Complete your diary. Write ONE word for each space. There is an example at the beginning (0).

Yesterday was a (**0**) …*busy*… day for me. I met Huck (**1**) ………… Cardiff Hill and we talked (**2**) ………… our secret. We're both (**3**) ………… of Injun Joe and we can't tell anyone (**4**) ………… true story. We (**5**) ………… to the jail and took some food (**6**) ………… poor old Muff. He was happy to see us. Today was the day of the (**7**) ………… . I don't like trials! The lawyer asked (**8**) ………… a lot of questions. I wore my Sunday clothes and they were terribly uncomfortable. I had to tell the truth about Injun Joe because it was the right thing to do. Now everyone in St Petersburg (**9**) ………… proud of me.

KEY • PREPARATION

3. READING AND WRITING PART 1 • Which notice (a-h) says this (1-5)? There is an example at the beginning (0).

0. ...*h*...   You can't talk to a teacher on Monday evenings.
1. ....   You must pay more for drinks.
2. ....   You can buy fishing equipment for half the price this week.
3. ....   Something important happened here.
4. ....   Your four-year-old child doesn't need to buy a ticket.
5. ....   You can't take your dog here.

a

DANGER!
High water on the river
Do not cross the bridge!

b

LIBERTY JOE'S
RESTAURANT
Since 1789
All you can eat for only $1.00!
Drinks not included

c

HISTORICAL SITE
Battle of Slim Buttes
September 1876

d

ST PETERSBURG PUBLIC LIBRARY
Silence at all times, please!
No pets allowed

e

JACK'S FISHING SHOP
50% off all camping
and fishing equipment
This week only!

f

MISSISSIPPI STEAMBOAT LINE
Ticket office open every day
7 am to 8 pm
Children under 6 travel free!

g

AUNT POLLY'S JAM SHOP
All jams are made by hand!
Closed on Sundays and
holidays

h

ST PETERSBURG
SCHOOL
Meetings for parents
& teachers
Every Wednesday at 7 pm

1. PICTURE SUMMARY • Look at the pictures from *The Adventures of Tom Sawyer* below. They are not in the right order. Put them in the order in which they appear in the story.

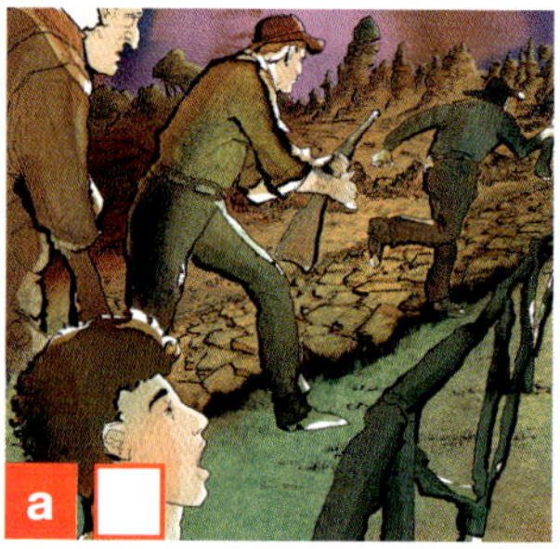

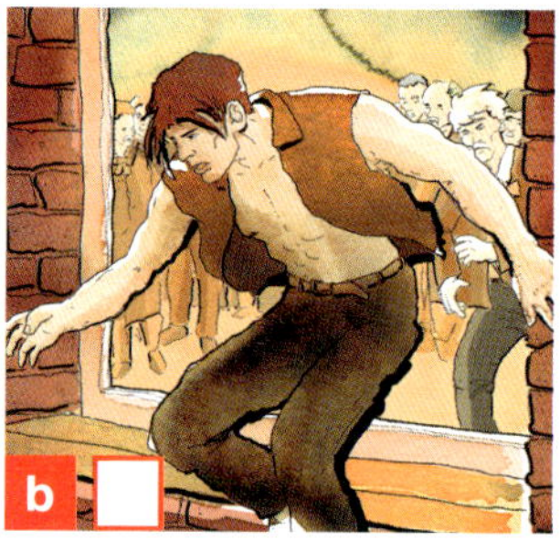

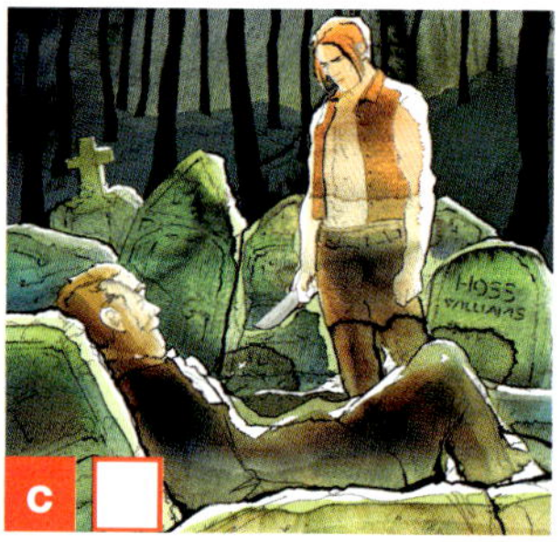

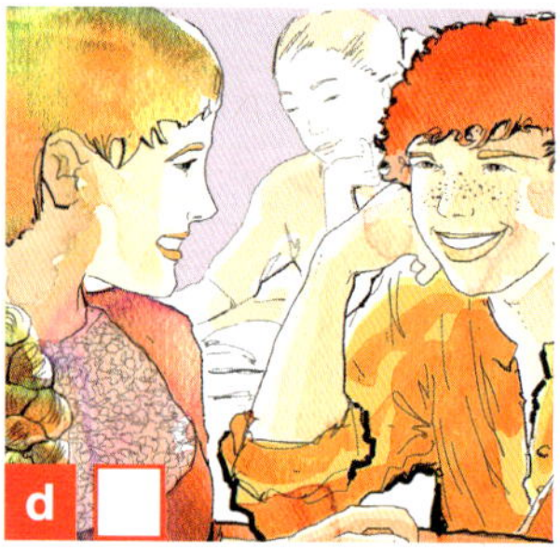

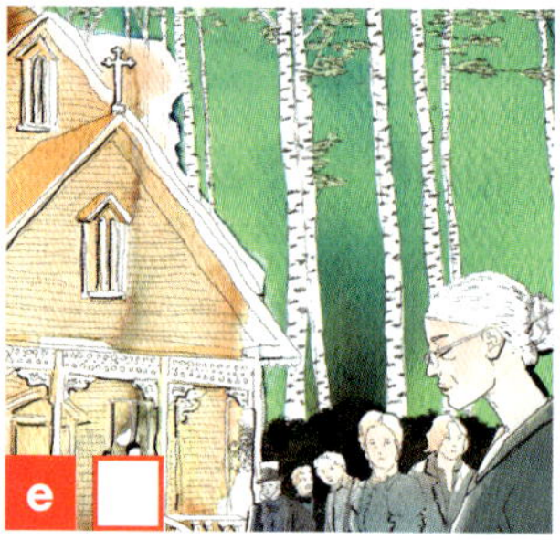

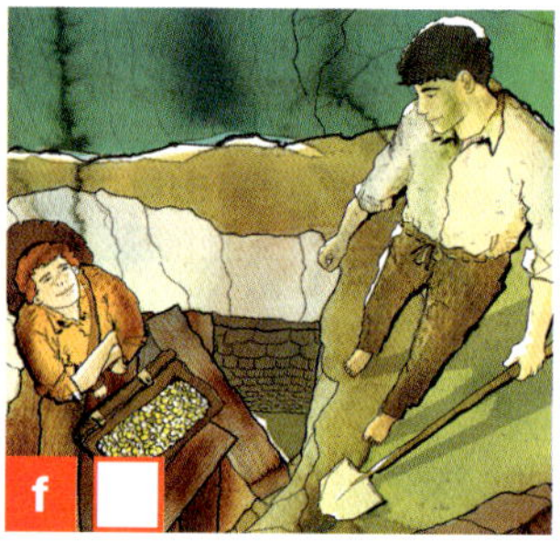

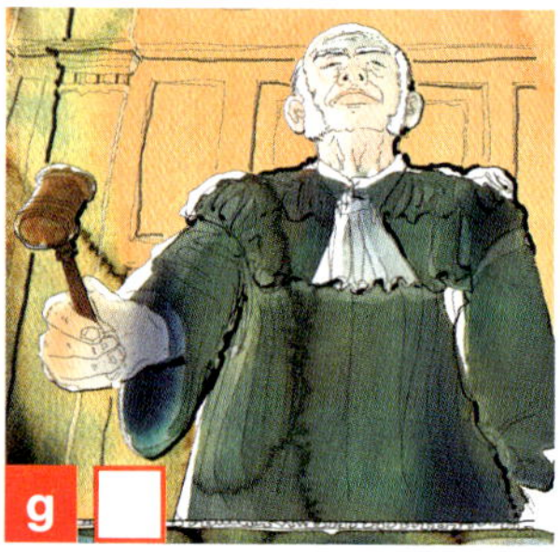

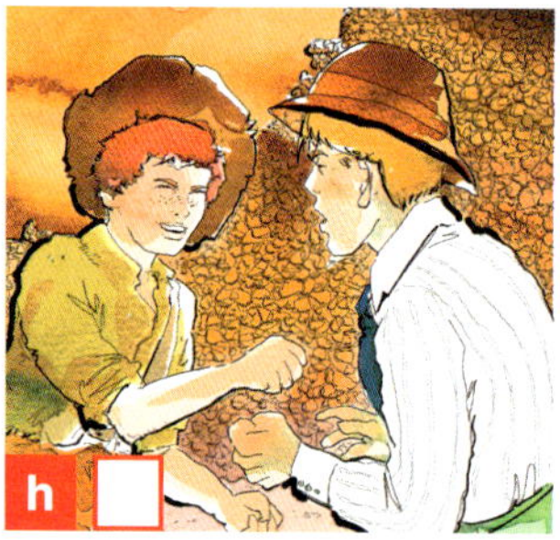

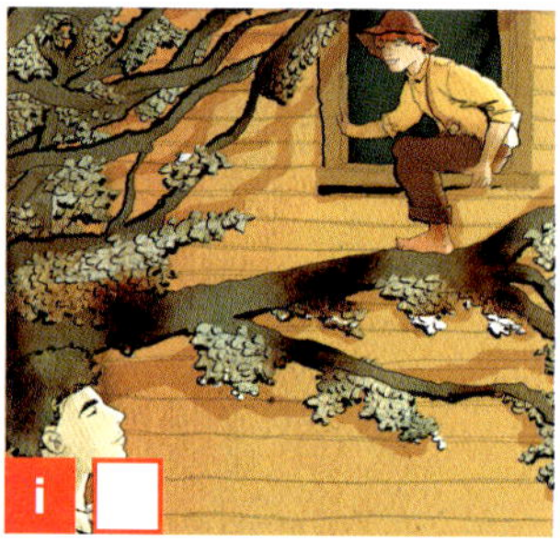

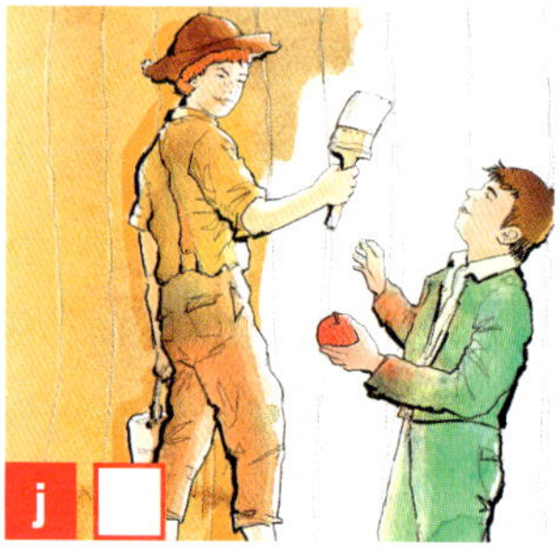

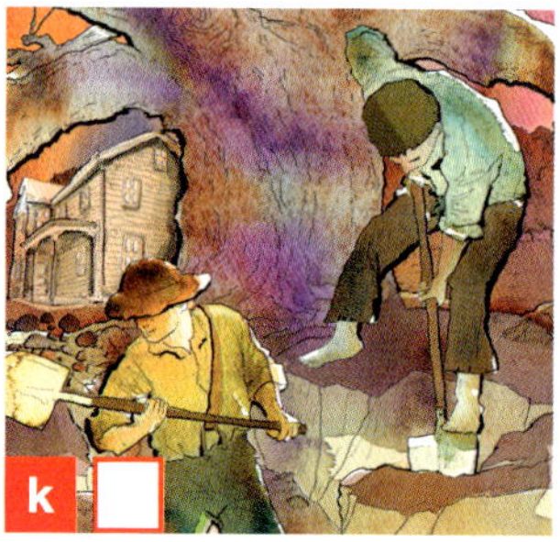

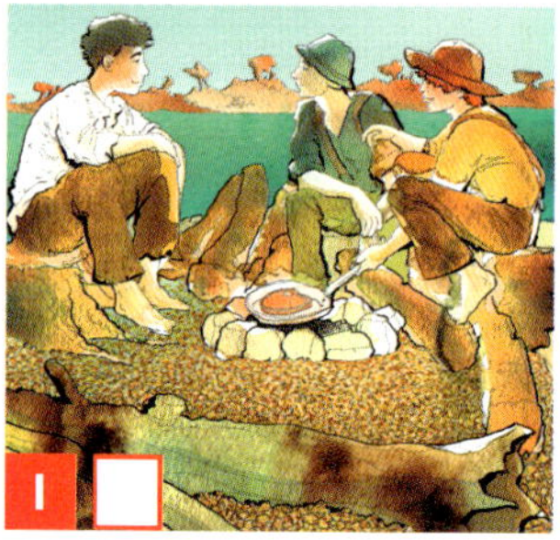

LET'S REVISE THE STORY

2. WHO WAS IT? • Match the description with the character. You can use a name more than once.

> Muff Potter • Huck Finn • Joe Harper •
> Mrs Hopkins • Becky Thatcher • Sid • Injun Joe •
> Aunt Polly • Dr Robinson • Tom Sawyer

1. She was a witch. ....
2. She looked after Tom. ....
3. He didn't have a family. ....
4. She was very pretty. ....
5. He was Tom's brother. ....
6. He went to Jackson's Island with Tom and Huck. ....
7. He killed Doctor Robinson. ....
8. He went to jail. ....
9. He was always bored at Sunday School. ....
10. He never went to school. ....
11. He brought a black beetle to church. ....
12. He hid a treasure in McDougal's Cave. ....
13. He wasn't invited to Becky's birthday picnic. ....
14. He studied dead bodies. ....

3. WHAT ABOUT YOU? • Answer these questions.

1. What was your favorite part of the story?
   ....
2. Who was your favorite character and why?
   ....
3. Which character didn't you like?
   ....
4. Which other story by Mark Twain would you like to read?
   ....

VALUES & FEELINGS

 ## THINK!

1 Which values and feelings do you think each chapter is about? Go back to each chapter and find the words that describe how people feel, what people do and what is important to them. Then complete the table below.

Chapters 1-2 ▶ *smart* | ....

Chapters 3-4 | .... | ....

Chapters 5-6 | .... | *helpful*

Chapter 7 | ....

 ## THE CHARACTERS

2 Use the words in the box to describe the characters below.

friendly • violent • clever • honest • lazy • funny • bad • angry • brave • unkind • dangerous • responsible • caring • helpful • kind • free • intelligent • different • afraid • a good friend • worried • poor • alone • strong • sad

THE STORY

(3) In the word cloud you can see words that describe how people feel – their feelings. Which feelings can you find in *The Adventures of Tom Sawyer*? Look at the word cloud below and divide them into "good feelings" and "bad feelings", and say why.

violent sad proud
caring lost free friendly
happy hopeful angry
excited frightened pleased
worried kind helpful
unkind

GOOD FEELINGS

....
....
....
....

BAD FEELINGS

....
....
....
....

 YOUR TURN!

(4) What about you? Prepare your own word cloud using the words above. Make them big if they are important to you. Make them small if they aren't important to you.

Your word cloud

This reader uses the **EXPANSIVE READING** approach: where reading is not only the enjoyment of the story and the discovery of a new language, but an opportunity to make cultural connections.

The new language introduced in this step of our **Green Apple Life Skills** series is listed below and language from lower steps is included, too.

For a complete list of all three steps, see *The Black Cat Graded Readers Handbook* at *blackcat-cideb.com*.

STEP ONE A2

Verb tenses
Past Simple; Past Continuous; Future reference: *will*

Verb forms and patterns
Regular and common irregular verbs; Passive forms: Present Simple and Past Simple with very common verbs (e.g. *made, called, born*)

Modal verbs
Could: ability, requests;
Will: future reference, offers, promises, predictions;
May (present and future reference): possibility;
Mustn't: prohibition;
Have (got) to: external obligation

Types of clause
Subordination after *if* (zero and 1st conditionals); Defining relative clauses with: *who, where*

Other
Comparative and superlative of adjectives (regular and irregular); Formation of adverbs (regular and irregular)

Step One
If you enjoyed this reader, try another one in Step One...

- *The Prince and the Pauper*, by Mark Twain **(Life Skills)**
- *Great Expectations*, by Charles Dickens
- *The Bottle Imp*, by Robert L. Stevenson

Step Two
...or take a step forward to Step Two!

- *Adventures of Huckleberry Finn*, by Mark Twain
- *Tales from Camelot*, by Victoria Heward **(Life Skills)**
- *Oliver Twist*, by Charles Dickens